DUMPTY

THE AGE OF TRUMP IN VERSE

JOHN LITHGOW

CHRONICLE PRISM

Library of Congress Cataloging-in-Publication Data

Names: Lithgow, John, 1945- author, illustrator.
Title: Dumpty : the age of Trump in verse / John Lithgow.
Description: [1st edition]. | San Francisco : Chronicle Books, [2019]. |
Summary: "Award-winning actor and bestselling author John Lithgow wields a whip-smart, satirical pen in this poetic diatribe chronicling the last few abysmal years in politics. With lacerating wit, he takes readers verse by verse through the history of Donald Trump's presidency, lampooning the likes of Betsy DeVos, Anthony Scaramucci, Scott Pruitt, Paul Manafort, Trump's doctors, and many others. Illustrated from cover to cover with Lithgow's never-before-seen line drawings, the poems collected in Dumpty draw inspiration from A. A. Milne, Lewis Carroll, Edward Lear, Rodgers and Hammerstein, Mother Goose, and many more. A YUGE feat of laugh-out-loud lyrical storytelling, this hilarious and timely volume is bound to bring joy to poetry lovers, political junkies, and Lithgow fans"— Provided by publisher.
Identifiers: LCCN 2019026339 (print) | LCCN 2019026340 (ebook) | ISBN 9781452182759 (hardcover) | ISBN 9781797201405 (ebook)
Subjects: LCSH: Trump, Donald, 1946—Humor. | Trump, Donald, 1946—Caricatures and cartoons. | Trump, Donald, 1946—Poetry. | Political satire, American. | Humorous poetry, American. | American wit and humor. | United States—Politics and government—2017—Humor.
Classification: LCC E913.3 .L58 2019 (print) | LCC E913.3 (ebook) | DDC 973.93302/07—dc23
LC record available at https://lccn.loc.gov/2019026339
LC ebook record available at https://lccn.loc.gov/2019026340

Manufactured in the United States of America.

Illustrations by John Lithgow.
Design by Sara Schneider.
Typesetting by Happenstance Type-O-Rama.
Typeset in Adobe Caslon, Brandon Grotesque, and Daft Brush.

10 9 8 7 6 5 4 3

CHRONICLE PRISM

Chronicle Prism is an imprint of Chronicle Books LLC,
680 Second Street, San Francisco, California 94107
chronicleprism.com

"I know words. I have the best words. But there's no better word than stupid. Right?"

DUMPTY, DECEMBER 30, 2015

CONTENTS

INTRODUCTION

I always knew I'd be preaching to the choir. Slap the title *DUMPTY* on a book of political humor and your bias is glaringly obvious. From the beginning I have intended these verses for people who oppose our current president, hoping to briefly yank them out of their chronic depression at his persistent grip on executive power.

But I'm a professional actor as well as an amateur satirist. When I act, I never restrict myself to preaching to the choir. I want to please everybody. I try to make audiences laugh, cry, or scream and to occasionally make them think. I'm an equal opportunity entertainer: if I'm onstage and you're out front, I'm your man.

Alas, with political humor, pleasing everybody is impossible. Show your bias and you're guaranteed to piss off half the crowd. So as an introduction to my first book of political satire, let me briefly turn away from the choir and address myself to all you Friends of Dumpty out there. You FODs may have already judged my book by its cover and refused to even open it, but if you're reading these words, read on: I'm talking to you.

My dear fellow citizens,

Though I myself can't fathom it, I acknowledge your sincere devotion to Dumpty, that strange, splenetic man. I see you on TV, laughing, cheering, and chanting at his rallies. You stand in line beforehand for hours on end, primed for the time of your lives. In your eyes, Dumpty's bullying is courage, his bigotry is patriotism, his vulgarity is authenticity, his cruelty is unbridled fun. Your support for him springs from sheer infatuation, and like most infatuations, it's incomprehensible to everyone else. It's certainly incomprehensible to me.

But let me ask you a few questions, and promise that you'll answer truthfully:

Given that Dumpty is such a crude, paranoid, petulant, cowardly, vicious liar, con man, and crook, would you want to work in an office where he was in charge? Would you want to join his downtrodden White House staff or the weird cast of characters in his cabinet? Would you want him to invest your life savings for you? Would you want to sit next to him at a dinner party, picnic, or sporting event? Would you want to carpool or (God forbid!) drive cross-country with him? Would you hire him to babysit your toddler or fix him up with your best friend's daughter? Would you ask him to speak at your own memorial service?

If you answer no to all of these questions (and how could you not?) then why in the world would you entrust your country's future and the future of this fragile planet to him? Pause for a moment and contemplate your own contradictory leanings.

Crazy, right?

Now. Hopefully I've jostled your state of mind just enough for you to take a peek at my poems. Don't worry: if you honestly think that my politics stink and I flout your redoubtable strictures, then kick off your shoes, mix your favorite drink, screw the words, and just look at the pictures.

JL, June 9, 2019

TRUMPTY DUMPTY

Trumpty Dumpty wanted a wall
To stir up a rabid political brawl.
His Republican rivals, both feckless and stodgy,
Succumbed in the end to his rank demagogy.

Dumpty's wall made no earthly sense,
A boondoggle built at enormous expense.
But he promised, in speeches despotic and shrill,
He'd make certain that Mexico footed the bill.

Trumpty Dumpty kept insisting.
More and more citizens started resisting.
Sadly, there won't be an end to this tale,
At least until reasonable people prevail.

In January 2017, **DONALD J. TRUMP** *became the 45th president of the United States.*

THE PRESIDENT'S PAGEANT

In his oval-shaped snuggery, Dumpty reclined
On a break from Fake News and sharp censure.
He had waited all day for a chance to unwind
By recalling his flashiest venture:

An evening in Russia, 2013,
That he'd scarcely dared even imagine.
Each nation had chosen its own beauty queen
For his Moscow Miss Universe Pageant.

Dumpty's grandest pet project had come to fruition,
His gaudiest spectacle yet.
And those hookers displaying their bold micturition,
Was something he'd never forget.

"I've got it!" cried Dumpty while bolting upright.
"A reprise of my old avocation!
A *President's Pageant* held right here on site!
And the East Room's the perfect location!

"Miss Universe? No! Not this time around.
I'm done with Macron, May, and Merkel.
America First! One of *ours* will be crowned!
And perhaps from my own inner circle.

"For starters, Ivanka's superior air
Can't obscure her demure sensuality.
And Tiffany, too (though she hasn't a prayer),
Is a lock for Miss Congeniality.

"Picture Hicks in the spotlight! A radiant vision!
That body, that hair, and those eyes.
And Hope would mop up in the Talent Division
With her skill at inventing white lies.

"Louise Linton, Mnuchin's voluptuous bride,
Would love to compete with this set.
She'd appear like an empress, with Steve at her side,
Flown in on a Treasury jet.

"Omarosa's a looker who'd light up the stage
With diversity, danger, and sass.
She would hopefully deal with her issues of rage
Once we've reactivated her pass.

"By rights, Kirstjen Nielsen should join the parade.
She's blonde, statuesque, and beguiling.
But the toll of the cold-blooded role she has played
Tends to prevent her from smiling.

"Kellyanne comes to mind as another suggestion,
Though not in the interview portions,
For she'd bulldoze her judge in the midst of a question,
With alternative facts and distortions.

"Two contestants at last would stride onto the green
To a fanfare performed on a bugle.
Their fame is gigantic (though not squeaky clean):
Stormy Daniels and Karen McDougal.

"One would certainly win, one would take second place,
With the others all clustering around them.
But in spite of her usual coolness and grace,
The first lady's unlikely to crown them."

Dumpty savored this fantasy, sighing out loud
As the fire flickered out in the grate.
The dazzling beauties and sparkling crowd
Had eclipsed all the burdens of state.

He banished all thoughts of the Washington scene,
Of his poll numbers rapidly falling.
Of Manafort, Cohen, of Rod Rosenstein,
Of the deafening roar of the Mueller machine.
In producing a pageant and picking a queen,
He had finally found his true calling.

Donald Trump produced the 62nd Miss Universe pageant in Moscow in November 2013, the same time the salacious "golden shower" incident involving Trump allegedly took place at a Moscow hotel.

HOPE HICKS *was the White House communications director from August 2017 to March 2018.* **OMAROSA MANIGAULT NEWMAN** *is a former political aide to President Donald Trump.*

KIRSTJEN NIELSEN, *appointed U.S. secretary of homeland security in December 2017, is known for enacting the family separation policy along the Mexican border. After Corey Lewandowski and Paul Manafort left Trump's 2016 presidential campaign,* **KELLYANNE CONWAY** *became campaign manager, and later, in 2017, presidential counselor.*

The American pornographic actress, stripper, and director **STEPHANIE CLIFFORD**, *known professionally as Stormy Daniels, alleged she had an affair with Trump in 2006 and was paid by Michael Cohen, Trump's former lawyer, to keep quiet ahead of the 2016 election. Former* Playboy *model* **KAREN MCDOUGAL** *allegedly had a nine-month affair with Trump.*

AN EX-LIEUTENANT GENERAL
(AFTER GILBERT AND SULLIVAN)

I am the very model of an ex-lieutenant general.
Although my reputation is decidedly ephemeral.
In spite of all my service in remote Afghani-stin afore;
No officer has screwed the pooch as much as Michael Flynn-afore.

When President Obama made me head of all things clandestine,
He realized he'd brought to life a governmental Frankenstein.
But then I made a killing in a case of public pillory
By shouting "Lock her up!" in my harangue opposing Hillary.

So Dumpty made me National Security Advisor-y
Until I let the crafty Russian secret service hire me.
Then I became the target of a Special Counsel crime report,
A fate I shared with Cohen, Donald Jr., and with Manafort.

I plead the Fifth Amendment when the arbiters of law attack
My meeting Jared Kushner in a room with Sergey Kislyak.
Although my reputation is decidedly ephemeral,
I am the very model of an ex-lieutenant general.

MICHAEL FLYNN *is a retired U.S. Army lieutenant general. He served as Donald Trump's national security advisor from January 2017 until he was dismissed in February 2017. In December of that year, he pleaded guilty to lying to the FBI.*

MY FAVORITE LIES
(AFTER RODGERS AND HAMMERSTEIN)

Muslim festivities on 9/11,
Barring the Russians has screwed the G7,
China makes none of my cheap merchandise:
These are a few of my favorite lies.

Records were smashed at my inauguration,
I nailed Korean denuclearization,
I'll be awarded the Nobel Peace Prize:
These are a few of my favorite lies.

I, only I, am the working man's savior,
Knew not a word of Mike Flynn's misbehavior,
Comey infested my campaign with spies:
These are a few of my favorite lies.

When *The Times* bites,
When *The Post* stings,
When I'm feeling sad,
I simply remember my favorite lies
And then I don't feel so bad.

Collusion with Putin's a Fake News aspersion,
Tahoe was merely a golfing excursion,
Justice was served with those Central Park guys:
These are a few of my favorite lies.

Anarchy reigns on the streets of Chicago,
No taint of corruption befouls Mar-a-Lago,
Earth is unharmed when the temperatures rise:
These are a few of my favorite lies.

Hillary once had a fling with Osama,
A stork from Nairobi delivered Obama,
Things are improved when democracy dies:
These are a few of my favorite lies.

When the Law bites,
When the Truth stings,
When I'm feeling blue,
I simply remember my favorite lies
Then I can con all

Of

You.

---

*Among many of Donald Trump's "alternative facts" documented by
the media, Trump claimed to have had record-breaking crowds on
the National Mall during his inauguration, despite photographic
evidence to the contrary. During one of his rallies in 2015, Trump
claimed that thousands of New Jersey Muslims celebrated the 9/11
attacks; there is no evidence to support this allegation. While President
Trump advocated for the importance of "made in America" goods,
many Trump-branded products are manufactured in countries like
China, Indonesia, and Turkey.*

DANCING WITH THE STAR

"Please, Mr. President, keep to the point,"
Said the POTUS's weary advisor.
"We've been waiting for weeks on your cabinet picks
And no one is any the wiser."

"Winning was fun," Dumpty said with a scowl
As he muted the sound on Fox News.
"But if I had known how much work this would be,
I'd have probably chosen to lose."

The aide drummed his fingers and knitted his brow.
"Throw out some ideas," he said.
"Just picture, for starters, the person you'd like
As Department of Energy head."

"Rick Perry!" cried Dumpty. "I saw him last week!
Dancing cha-cha on network TV!
He's tremendous! And frankly a beautiful choice
For livening up D of E!"

"Him?" gasped the aide. "But didn't he claim
That he'd have the department disbanded?
He'd be like an admiral plotting to sink
Every ship in the fleet he commanded."

"Tremendous!" said POTUS. "A beautiful scheme
For cutting out waste and expense!
We'll use it to fill *all* the cabinet chairs!
(Though perhaps not the one for Defense)."

"But sir," the aide stammered, "the press would go ape.
The announcement would spark pandemonium!
The department's in charge of our missiles and subs,
Of our nukes and our stolen plutonium."

"Well, sure," Dumpty grumbled. "Rick's not quite equipped
With a nuclear physicist's brain.
But you're looking for Energy? Check out his moves!
He struts like a rutting Great Dane!"

"I'm afraid," said the aide, "there's too much information
That Perry can't possibly know.
And besides, your opinion is based on his stint
On a cheesy reality show."

"Screw it!" barked Dumpty. "I've made up my mind!
Your help is no longer required.
I got where I am on account of TV.
Reality series are my pedigree.
When you shit on Rick Perry, you're shitting on me!
We're done here! I've had it! *YOU'RE FIRED*!!"

Former Texas governor **JAMES RICHARD "RICK" PERRY** *was eliminated from ABC's* Dancing with the Stars *in September 2016. While campaigning for president in 2012, he promised to abolish the Department of Energy. In December 2016, President Trump made Perry the fourteenth U.S. secretary of energy.*

SCARAMOUCHE

The Italians created a classic buffoon
Who was cowardly, boastful, and louche,
A scoundrel whom everyone else would lampoon:
That slippery scamp *Scaramouche*!

In this day and age, should this rascal appear
With his posture both craven and brash,
He would probably choose the political sphere
After piling up mountains of cash.

The White House might possibly find him a place,
Making use of his tart turn of phrase.
But alas, Scaramouche would then fall on his face
After only eleven short days.

For he'd shock us with language beyond indiscreet
Like a sailor or potty-mouthed jock.
For example, he'd boast of the unlikely feat
Of "not trying to suck my own cock."

Scaramouche would depart to perfunctory applause,
An absurd tragicomic creation,
Recalled, if at all, for his colorful flaws
'Til he mugs for the next generation.

In fact, he was here! We all caught his act!
All that cocky and crass hootchy-kootchy.
His creaky old antics are all still intact:
For Scaramouche, we've had Scaramucci!

ANTHONY SCARAMUCCI *is a financier and entrepreneur.
He served as Donald Trump's White House communications direc-
tor for eleven days, before Trump fired him on July 31, 2017.*

25

RUB-A-DUB-DUB
(AFTER MOTHER GOOSE)

Rub-a-dub-dub
Three men in a tub,
And who do you think they be?
Harold Bornstein, Tom Price,
And Rear Admiral Jackson,
All sharing the title "MD."

Doctor Bornstein, for one,
Is a figure of fun,
Though he's cared for the Head of Our Nation.
He expounded at length
On the president's strength
As he read a verbatim dictation.

The POTUS's hair
Got particular care
(Orange locks were his signature feature).
But poor Bornstein was hosed
When we learned he'd imposed
A daily regime of Propecia.

Tom Price was a stealth
Secretary of Health,
Sneaking off under cover of night.
He was bland as vanilla
But fierce as Attila
On behalf of the Radical Right.

Though anti-elitist,
This ex-orthopedist
Saw his power and position unravel.
What caused this curtailment?
A plutocrat's ailment:
An addiction to private air travel.

Ronny Jackson's position
As White House physician
Gave him access to pills by the ton.
He would dole them out freely,
Patrolling genteelly
The horde while on board Air Force One.

He was tapped anyway
To head up the VA.
No one bothered to heed the Code Red.
His promotion suspended,
This admiral ended
In water way over his head.

Rub-a-dub-dub,
Three men in a tub.
Their professional prospects had fled.
They practiced no more
And when reaching the shore,
Took two aspirins and went straight to bed.

HAROLD BORNSTEIN *served as Donald Trump's personal physician for thirty-eight years. Trump cut ties with him after the doctor revealed that Trump took a prescription hair-growth medicine.*

TOM PRICE *was the secretary of health and human services under Donald Trump from February to September 2017, when he resigned after it was revealed that he had spent over $1 million of government funds for travel on private jets and military planes.*

Former physician to the president **RONNY JACKSON** *was nominated by President Trump as secretary of veterans affairs in March 2018. The next month, Jackson withdrew his name from consideration after allegations spread regarding his handling of prescription drugs, among other things. Trump appointed Jackson as his chief medical advisor in February 2019.*

THE GENTLEMEN OF THE DEFENSE

At first, the most promising partnership goin'
Was Cobb, Dowd, diGenova, Kasowitz & Cohen.

But rarely have lawyers made such a poor showin'
As Cobb, Dowd, diGenova, Kasowitz & Cohen.

Empty threats and deceptions were constantly flowin'
From Cobb, Dowd, diGenova, Kasowitz & Cohen.

But few legal experts paid heed to the crowin'
Of Cobb, Dowd, diGenova, Kasowitz & Cohen.

In time, the team's case proved extremely rough goin'
For Cobb, Dowd, diGenova, Kasowitz & Cohen.

They sensed, one by one, whence the cold wind was blowin'
Did Cobb, Dowd, diGenova, Kasowitz & Cohen.

So, besmirched by the towel each decided to throw in,
Off went Cobb, Dowd, diGenova, Kasowitz & Cohen.

And a new gang stepped up, dressed in rumpled Armani:
Giuliani, Giuliani, Giuliani & Giuliani.

TY COBB, **JOHN DOWD**, **JOSEPH DIGENOVA, MARC KASOWITZ**, *and* **MICHAEL COHEN** *all served as legal advisors to Donald Trump. In April 2018,* **RUDY GIULIANI** *joined Trump's personal legal team.*

THE LITTLE MAN WHO'S NOT ALL THERE

(AFTER WILLIAM HUGHES MEARNS)

Today, upon a White House stair,
I met a man who's not all there.
A Dumpty aide from opening day,
I wish, I wish he'd go away.

With ghostly face and sleepy eyes,
A hairless dome and furtive guise,
One thinks of him less as a policy maker
And more as an unctuous undertaker.

In public, whenever he's heard or seen,
He rants like a manic spin machine.
So there he sits, as if chained to a pillar,
His first name is Stephen, his last name is Miller.

By now his peers have all been canned,
But Dumpty insists he stay close at hand
To sate the POTUS's nativist urges
And launch his draconian immigrant purges.

Speechwriting, too, is a muscle he's flexed
(Although Dumpty rarely pays heed to the text).
Ramping up fears and trampling on hope
Made "American carnage" a Dumptyan trope.

For Miller, fidelity means blind devotion:
When Dumpty invents, he seconds the motion.
Post-election, for instance, he lied in his throat,
Claiming three million migrants had skewered the vote.

That pales beside Miller's most barbarous plan,
His blatantly racist and rash travel ban.
Of crazy ideas, the craziest of all:
The wall! The wall! The beautiful wall!

But what does he see as his crowning achievement?
His masterpiece of abuse and bereavement?
Zero tolerance! Immigrant children abducted,
In a program that Miller himself had constructed.

Along with the skipper of our ship of state,
He holds in his hands our precarious fate.
Together they sail on the seas of autocracy.
Heaven watch over our fragile democracy.

Tomorrow I fear, on that same White House stair,
The same little man once again will be there.
Once again he'll be there on the following day.
I wish, I wish he'd go away.

A "White House survivor," **STEPHEN MILLER** *is a speechwriter and one of the longest-tenured political advisors for Donald Trump, serving since January 2017.*

REEB-A-DEEP-DEEP

Reeb-a-deep-deep
Four men in a jeep.
No wonder they look so annoyed.
They're McMaster and Kelly
And Mattis and Flynn:
Four generals, all unemployed.

Flynn was a snake
And a man on the take,
Russia's unwitting dupe from the start.
A self-immolator
And close to a traitor,
Of the four he was first to depart.

His stolid successor,
A soldier-professor,
Was a champ at averting disaster.
But inviting our doom,
Dumpty lowered the boom
On the stoical H. R. McMaster.

John Kelly's arrival
Betokened survival,
But he was embattled as well.
When at last he stepped down,
He blew Crazytown
Like a prisoner sprung from his cell.

The last of the four
To head out the door
Was the flinty and fearsome Jim Mattis.
His tenure a bust,
Mad Dog left in disgust.
Heaven help our defense apparatus.

Reeb-a-deep-deep
Four men in a jeep,
Dumped by Dumpty, the worst of his species.
Their honor is lost
For they've learned at their cost:
All he touches he turns into feces.

H. R. MCMASTER *is a retired U.S. Army general who served as Donald Trump's national security advisor from February 2017 to April 2018.*

JOHN F. KELLY *is a retired U.S. Marine Corps general who served as secretary of homeland security under Donald Trump until he was appointed White House chief of staff in July 2017, a position he left after eighteen months.*

JIM MATTIS *is a retired U.S. Marine Corps general who served as the secretary of defense from January 2017 until December 2018, when he retired due to policy differences with Donald Trump.*

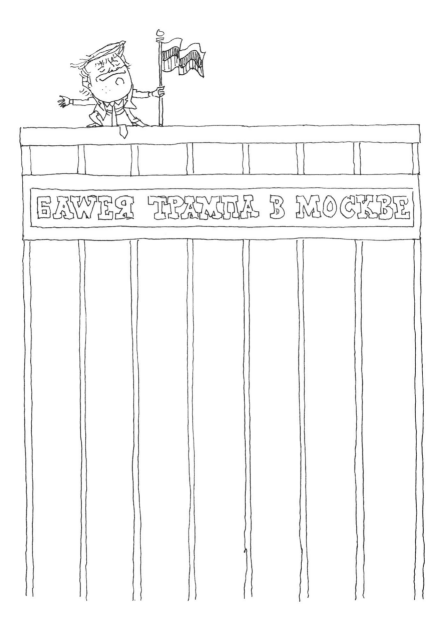

TRUMPTY DUMPTY: PART 2

Trumpty Dumpty wanted a tower
To showcase his personal glory and power.
But Putin came up with a devilish plot
To exploit Dumpty's dream for covert *kompromat*.

Dumpty proceeded with Cohen and Sater,
Ignoring the possible label of "traitor."
When thereafter their dealings were open to all,
The odds were that Dumpty would have a great fall.

A business associate of Trump, **FELIX SATER** *is a Russian-American ex-felon who had ties to organized crime. He worked with Michael Cohen on a plan to build a Trump Tower in Moscow in 2015 and 2016. Cohen later admitted that the licensing deal for Trump Tower Moscow continued after Trump secured the Republican nomination.*

ALL AT SEA

(AFTER JOHN MASEFIELD)

I must go down to the seas again,
   To the lonely sea and sun.
I've got a flotilla of ten big yachts
   And I'll pick my favorite one.
I'll lie on the deck all slathered in oil,
   Sipping a frosty libation,
And think of all of the things I can do
   To privatize education.

I must go down to the seas again
   (More specifically, down to Lake Erie).
With a sea captain's eyes, I'll boldly devise
   My own educational theory:
A nationwide network of new charter schools
   Where Calvinist thought is enshrined.
The children whose parents can't manage the cost
   Will have to be left behind.

In my stateroom, afloat on the seas again,
   I'll dine on exotic cuisines.
I'll choose all my cooks from a rarefied group:
   Ex for-profit university deans.
They'll counsel me, too, using knowledge they've gained
   From running their various schools,
For example, suggesting that I should roll back
   All Obama's ridiculous rules.

When I sail in from the seas again,
   I'll tend to more pressing affairs,
Like arming American teachers with guns
   To protect them from grizzly bears.
I'll pick some new clothes and accessories
   And back to the seas I'll go,
Since all at sea has tended to be
   My usual status quo.

With no experience as a public school student, teacher, principal, superintendent, or administrator, **BETSY DEVOS** *assumed office as the secretary of education on February 7, 2017.*

SIC TRANSIT

Head the EPA?
He wouldn't do it.
Back in Oklahoma
He'd wanted to screw it.
Fourteen times
He opted to sue it.
But when the new POTUS
Appointed him to it,
It was such a juicy bone,
He decided to chew it.

The agency's mission?
He sought to undo it.
Fossil-fuel industries
Were eager to cue it.
Climate change science?
He would blithely pooh-pooh it.
Environmentalist protest?
He tried to subdue it.
The new chief executive
Backed him all through it.

After six months in office,
He finally blew it.
Swampy behavior?
He didn't eschew it.
Donor-funded travel?
He'd way overdo it.
A Chick-fil-A suite?
His wife was into it.
Cheap housing from a lobbyist?

He chose to pursue it,
And a big-ticket phone booth
To block out the bruit.

Brazen corruption?

No matter how he'd skew it,
There's no other way to view it,
And everybody knew it.
As Ovid might construe it
(And not a soul will rue it):
Sic transit Scott Pruitt.

SCOTT PRUITT *served as administrator of the Environmental Protection Agency from February 2017 until July 2018, when he resigned in the face of fourteen federal investigations.*

Translation: Look at that jerk Pruitt.

MY LUCKY DAY: AUGUST 21, 2018

Today is the luckiest day of my life.
I've been charged with corruption, along with my wife.

You'd think all those counts from a Federal Grand Jury
Would trigger despondency, panic, or fury.

But no! A separate shock to the nation
Has spared me the country's irate condemnation:

The president's fixer and his campaign ex-chief
Have each been convicted and branded a thief.

The tale of two crooks at the height of their power
Eclipsed my indictment in less than an hour.

Since their verdicts explicitly implicate POTUS,
My crimes have completely escaped public notice.

Hence nobody heard of my bank overruns,
Of the cash that I stole from my own campaign funds,

Of resorting to bookkeeping falsification
To pay for my relatives' Italian vacation,

For dentistry, golf, for my bed-hopping habit,
For a ticket in coach for the family rabbit.

The pundits won't bother to give me the shaft
For my fiscal abuses and runaway graft.

No perp walk in newspaper photos for me!
No punch line for comics on late-night TV!

Let Cohen and Manafort go down in history;
Me and my wife? We're shrouded in mystery.

If I tell you our names when you finish this poem,
I bet that you'll answer, "Gee, sorry. Don't know 'em!"

No infamy, censure, abasement, or strife:
Today is the luckiest day of my life.

On August 21, 2018, Congressman **DUNCAN D. HUNTER** *and his wife,* **MARGARET JANKOWSKI**, *were indicted on charges of conspiracy, wire fraud, and violating campaign finance laws. Later that same day, Trump associate Michael Cohen pleaded guilty and Paul Manafort was found guilty in separate court proceedings. Despite the charges against him, Hunter was re-elected in November, 2018.*

THE OSTRICH'S LAMENT

The Manafort trial was a terrible shock
To me and my eastern South African flock.
For years we'd been bred for our feathers and meat
In dusty enclosures and god-awful heat.
Ungainly and ugly, we'd suffered such scorn
That most of us wished that we'd never been born.
A species that civilization forgot,
Contempt and disgust were the ostrich's lot.

But when word of Paul Manafort spread through the veldt,
We gaily discarded the hand we'd been dealt.
With one lavish purchase, he'd rescued our pride:
A sport jacket made from *an ostrich's hide*!
"Stupendous!" we crowed. "How dashing! How chic!
The priciest garb in the Bijan boutique!"
This high-rolling mogul was bound to ensure
A glorious future for ostrich couture.

But abasement, dishonor, and humiliation
Came close on the heels of our wild jubilation.
Manafort showed us his fat feet of clay,
A poster boy proving that crime doesn't pay.
Revealed as a monster of fiscal duplicity,
His sport jacket spawned catastrophic publicity.
With a crook as the ostrich's fashion bellwether,
Who would buy sportswear that featured our leather?

Gloom has befallen the old ostrich ranch.
We're nursing a wound that no surgeon can stanch.
Our moment of glory was gone in a flash,
Betrayed by the laundering of ill-gotten cash.
The felon's in prison and we're in disgrace,
Cursing the wiles of the vile human race.
From afar you can picture our unhappy band,
Each one of us sticking its head in the sand.

50

Donald Trump's former campaign chairman **PAUL MANAFORT** *has been sentenced to seven and a half years in federal prison for financial crimes, conspiracy to defraud the United States, and witness tampering. Manafort is expected to pay restitution of at least $6 million for taxes that he never paid.*

YOU ARE OLD, FATHER WILBUR

(AFTER LEWIS CARROLL)

"You are old, Father Wilbur," the young man said.
"We're ready to call the embalmers.
And yet you've accepted employment instead
As the new secretary of commerce."

"In my youth," Wilbur rasped, "it was always my mission
To buy and sell bankrupted firms.
I sell access instead in my current position
On vastly more lucrative terms."

"But sir!" cried the lad to the crafty old snake,
"Aren't you subject to strict regulations?
You've consistently failed to relinquish your stake
In the business of shady rogue nations."

"A despicable slur!" the old codger inveighed,
His eyes growing angry and viperous.
"Everyone gains from the profits I've made
In Moscow, Beijing, and in Cyprus!"

"And yet," the youth answered, "from all that I see,
The older you get, you grow bolder.
You've raided the till of your own LLC
And cheated both friend and shareholder."

"These wild accusations are making me ill!"
Blurted Wilbur, increasingly nettled.
"And even if maybe I stole a few mil,
Each time I was busted, I settled!"

"According to *Forbes*," the boy said with a taunt,
"You're a shockingly petty offender.
They say that departing a cheap restaurant,
You pocketed packets of Splenda."

"I'm done!" Wilbur shouted, in peevish distress,
"With your scoffs and contemptuous glares!
I get quite enough from the liberal press!
Be off, or I'll kick you downstairs!"

WILBUR ROSS *is an investor and the U.S. secretary of commerce.*

KAVANAUGHTY

Chosen to parse constitutional law,
He's Brett Kavanaugh.

A Bethesda-bred jock from elite Georgetown Prep,
He's Brett Kavanep.

Renowned for a weird predilection for beer,
He's Brett Kavaneer.

Beach blanket blowouts with PJ and Squee,
He's Brett Kavanee.

Connected forever with barfing and boofing,
He's Brett Kavanoofing.

A boozy assault on Christine Blasey Ford,
He's Brett Kavanord.

Waggling his dick in a Yale coed's face,
His Brett Kavanace.

Sifting through muck for Counselor Starr,
He's Brett Kavanarr.

Sitting on secrets for Cheney and Dubya,
He's Brett Kavanubya.

The Federalist Society's bright golden boy,
He's Brett Kavanoy.

Declaring a hit job by Bill and by Hillary,
He's Brett Kavanillary.

Unleashing a rant that outdid Justice Thomas,
He's Brett Kavanomas.

Backed in the end by the Senate Boys' Club,
He's Brett Kavanub.

Of all the fine judges that POTUS could choose
To sit in the company of Charles Evans Hughes
And Warren and Brennan and Brandeis and Marshall,
Magisterial jurists, wise and impartial,
Instead, Dumpty fingered this callow young cad,
The feeblest justice we'll ever have had.
Hardly the Solon our Founders foresaw,

He's Brett Kavanaugh.

President Donald Trump's nominee, Justice **BRETT KAVANAUGH**, *was confirmed to the Supreme Court in October 2018 despite allegations of sexual assault and misconduct.*

CHRISTINE BLASEY FORD, *a professor of psychology at Palo Alto University, accused Kavanaugh of sexual assault when the two were in high school during the 1980s. Kavanaugh also allegedly exposed himself to a Yale classmate, Deborah Ramirez, at a party during their freshman year.*

THE MORTIFICATION OF ELLIOTT BROIDY

Things keep getting worse for poor Elliott Broidy.
His greed and libido have proved unalloyed. He
Began by adhering to law and morality,
But now he's the emblem of lust and venality.
His strenuous leer and his corpulent girth
Have made him the butt of satirical mirth.
Who can blame us? Just look at the man's recent past,
Full of scandals befitting the late Thomas Nast.

His first misdemeanor the press barely mentions:
Bribing the guys who doled out New York pensions.
But then, like some spreading financial dysplasia,
He lobbied for crooks in Ukraine and Malaysia
And, mired in the geopolitical gutter,
He poisoned the well with our allies in Qatar.
Through it all, he was having the time of his life
As millions were lavished on him and his wife.

The GOP bosses were walking on air
When they made him their deputy fund-raising chair.
But imagine their shock when this lecherous clown,
This overweight Icarus came crashing down.
The cause of his sudden, precipitous fall?
The saddest and sleaziest reason of all:
The source from which all his calamities stem
Was that hoariest of narratives, *cherchez la femme!*

The man, you would think, was a little too old
To cavort with a winsome *Playboy* centerfold.
But an overabundance of power and money
Provides an old grizzly with plenty of honey.
A bear? More precisely an old Saint Bernard
Who bird-dogged a bunny named Shera Bechard.
Their tale has a title that's aptly tabloidy:
The Mortification of Elliott Broidy.

A deck chair awaits on his own ship of fools
For flouting the strictest Republican rules.
Rule number one: you must never impregnate
A mistress who's also a vengeful ex-Playmate.
And if it should happen, keep things in proportion:
Don't get mixed up in a girlfriend's abortion.
And Cohen! How could Elliott pick such a jerk?
Nondisclosure agreements are *known* not to work!

Along with a touch of distinct schadenfreudy,
We glean a few lessons from Elliott Broidy:
A grasping obsession with power and wealth
Is bad for the country and bad for your health;
And fate tends to play its most dastardly tricks
On grabby old lechers who think with their dicks.
Although he departs in disgrace and vainglory,
Take Elliott to heart and take heart from his story.

In 2017, **ELLIOTT B. BROIDY** *was deputy finance chairman of the Republican National Committee. He resigned in April 2018 after it was reported that he had paid a former* Playboy *Playmate $1.6 million to cover up their affair.*

THE WALRUS AND THE KLEPTOCRAT

(AFTER LEWIS CARROLL)

The streets all glowed with autumn light
   Beyond the palace door.
Inside, the glittering chandeliers
   Lit up the marble floor.
The Walrus and the Kleptocrat
   Plumbed the ways of war.

"The time has come," the Walrus said,
   "To follow different courses;
To talk of promises forsworn,
   Of schisms and divorces.
We're scrapping the pact that keeps in check
   Intermediate-Range Nuclear Forces."

The Kleptocrat, that wily cat,
   Suppressed a furtive leer.
"Oh, no!" he cried, and wiped away
   A crocodilian tear.
"The INF has kept us safe
   For lo, this many a year!"

In fact, he'd never backed the pact
   Nor followed its decrees,
But had built a secret missile force
   With surreptitious ease,
Enough to bring the NATO alliance
   Trembling to its knees.

The Kleptocrat eyed his oblivious prey
  With the gaze of a snake in the grass.
The Walrus thought he'd skunked his foe
  But had given him a pass,
Unwittingly planting a servile kiss
  On the Kleptocrat's rosy ass.

A year before, another scene
  Was every bit as hinky:
A meeting of two heads of state
  At a summit in Helsinki,
Where the Kleptocrat wrapped the Walrus's boss
  Around his little pinkie.

The shadows crept across Red Square,
  The sky began to redden.
The Walrus snuggled in his bed,
  His limbs were limp and leaden.
He smiled at how his day had gone,
  The global order he'd redrawn.
He dreamed at last of a golden dawn
  Of nuclear Armageddon.

JOHN BOLTON *became Donald Trump's national security advisor in April 2018. He advised the president to withdraw from the Intermediate-Range Nuclear Forces Treaty with Russia, which Trump did in February 2019. Many analysts say that Russia's previous nuclear weapons development, ordered by President* **VLADIMIR PUTIN**, *had already violated this treaty.*

JARED AND MOHAMMED

Jared and Mohammed were
A very lucky pair.
Their families were filthy rich
And each retained a share.

Jared's Dumpty's son-in-law,
Mohammed's dad's a king
Who rules the Saudi Royal House:
Ka-ching! Ka-ching! Ka-ching!

Jared came from real estate,
Mohammed, Saudi oil.
They set about to find a way
To be each other's foil.

With Jared lending White House cred,
Mohammed could convince
The family fold that he should hold
The title of crown prince.

And in return, Mohammed would
Prevail on all his minions
To force a Jared Peace Plan on
Those pesky Palestinians.

Jared pulled a string or two
And no one thought it odd
When Dumpty's first official visit
Took him to Riyadh.

Once there, the Saudis engineered
A freaky photo op,
With Dumpty fondling a globe
Beside Mohammed's pop.

With this, the fathers forged a bond
Both sacred and iconic,
Clueless that the whole wide world
Considered it moronic.

The sons concocted cushy deals
The fathers were ecstatic,
Displaying their devout embrace
Of all things plutocratic.

Their claims of future two-way trade
Were wildly optimistic,
In spite of talk the House of Saud
Was brutal and sadistic.

Jamal Khashoggi wrote it up,
Mohammed threw a fit.
He sent his goons to Istanbul
To execute a hit.

Inside the Saudi consulate,
The poor entrapped Jamal
Was strangled and dismembered by
The prince's cruel cabal.

Everybody everywhere
Declared it homicide,
But Dumpty and his son-in-law
Both took Mohammed's side.

Global disrepute encumbered
All their rosy plans,
For though Mohammed did the deed,
There's blood on Jared's hands.

Jared and Mohammed are
A most unlucky twosome.
They started bright and glistery
But now there's little mystery:
Their legacy in history
Is grisly, grim, and gruesome.

The crown prince of Saudi Arabia, **MOHAMMED BIN SALMAN**, *authorized a secret security force that committed multiple crimes in a campaign to silence dissenters, including, according to the CIA, the murder of* **JAMAL KHASHOGGI**, *a journalist and Saudi Arabian dissident.*

Intelligence reports on **JARED KUSHNER**, *Donald Trump's son-in-law and senior advisor, revealed that multiple foreign leaders targeted him, aiming to use him to advance their political and business interests.*

A LIBERAL'S COMPLAINT

Sean Hannity,
Sean Hannity.
You tidal wave of vanity!

You media profanity!
Purveying rank inanity
That verges on insanity!

You gross albino manatee!
With zero class, urbanity,
Bearing, nay *humanity*!

Your head is full of granity!
Your brain is mashed bananity!
You're such a horse's fannity!

Grow up! And be a mannity!
Or find another planet-y,
Sean Hannity.

SEAN HANNITY *is a conservative political radio and television host on the Fox News Channel.*

SEVEN DAYS IN NOVEMBER

The midterms had ended the evening before
When Dumpty confronted the White House press corps.
With his opening words he proclaimed "Total victory!"
But facts inconveniently proved contradictory:

The House had been flipped by the conquering Dems,
Including an army of crusading femmes,
And talk of impeachment was filling the air
With Schiff, Cummings, and Nadler each claiming a chair.

All at once Jim Acosta, Dumpty's CNN nemesis,
Provoked an explosion that rattled the premises.
His questioning triggered a Dumptyan roar
Like a bull at the hands of a deft picador.

In minutes, Acosta's press pass was suspended.
Reportorial norms were thus gravely upended.
"Total victory," that daft self-delusional phrase,
Had fueled the misrule of the next seven days.

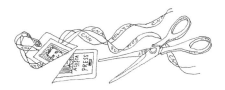

With the force of a rapidly moving monsoon,
Dumpty rashly reacted that midafternoon.
His target? The focus of all his obsessions,
His hapless AG, the beleaguered Jeff Sessions.

Poor Jeff was evicted in shame and disgrace,
Supplanted by someone that no one could place:
Matthew Whitaker, master of self-reinvention,
Whose right-wing harangues had caught Dumpty's attention.

This Washington horse of a different color
Saw red on the subject of Robert S. Mueller.
So what was his primary qualification?
His promise to quash Mueller's investigation.

Hence Dumpty had managed in one single day
To doubly debase the American Way:
Two crimes in plain sight to appall and disgust us,
Breach of Free Press and Obstruction of Justice.

Day two, with these Dumpty debacles behind him,
The walls of the White House no longer confined him.
His people thought, lest his morale should unravel,
They'd send him abroad for a few days of travel.

The principal leaders of each western nation
Were shortly to meet for a French convocation.
A century had passed since the Great War concluded
And POTUS's staff wanted Dumpty included.

A weekend in France, they thought, might do him good.
Paris for certain, but first Belleau Wood:
A centenary tribute with speeches and song,
A salute to dead veterans! What could go wrong!

A prediction of rainfall gave Dumpty a scare.
He feared its unsightly effect on his hair.
So while hundreds bore witness where multitudes fell,
Dumpty stayed dry in his Paris hotel.

This faux pas was met with a storm of contempt
From which most of his staff had thought Dumpty exempt.
They sought his redemption the following day
At a stately event on the Champs-Elysées.

He would march with his peers to a solemn memorial,
Dignified, humble, and ambassadorial.
If he kept a cool head and avoided a slip,
The prospects were rosy for righting the ship.

Unhappily, all of their hopes were in vain:
Paris was drenched with continuous rain.
Dumpty yielded once more to tonsorial anxiety,
Thus taking a pass on compassionate piety.

The procession went forward despite the deluge,
But the impact of POTUS's absence was huge.
While the others all marched, Dumpty rode in a car,
Igniting a storm of disastrous PR.

The climax of Dumpty's Parisian burlesque
Might well have been comic if it weren't so grotesque.
He had bickered with Merkel and blasted Macron,
Now they sat side by side, all civility gone.

When a shifty-eyed latecomer strode to the stand,
Teuton and Gaul coldly shook the man's hand.
But Dumpty lit up like a bright chandelier!
His friend had arrived! The beloved *Vladimir*!

Dumpty's foreign adventure was over that night,
A trip where not one single thing had gone right.
He slumped into the White House and staggered upstairs
Having learned that his strength was not Foreign Affairs.

Moonlight still shone on the broad White House lawn
As Dumpty awoke a few hours before dawn.
With his thoughts and emotions in wild disarray,
He strove to keep memories of Paris at bay.

But sadly, before he could pull on his pants,
New crises eclipsed the fiascos in France.
Unpacified by the comforts of home,
A long list of torments now cluttered his dome.

For starters Matt Whitaker, Dumpty's new hire,
Had come under virulent critical fire.
Unconfirmed by the Senate and prone to corruption,
His appointment was stirring frenetic disruption.

Meanwhile in Arabia, tempted by Mammon,
Dumpty had vouched for Mohammed bin Salman.
With an excess of greed and a dearth of remorse,
In the case of Khashoggi he'd backed the wrong horse.

And as fire in the West dealt out mass devastation,
Its victims heard Dumpty's inane explanation:
"Bad forest management! Stupid mistakes!
They say that all Finns are provided with rakes!"

In the midst of the day's cataclysmic commotion
Came news of the object of Dumpty's devotion:
Like another unmentionable government female,
Ivanka did classified work on her e-mail!

Sensing family strife and political harm,
Reporters had hastened to sound the alarm.
But Dumpty, immune to the pangs of hypocrisy,
Was deaf to this instance of rank idiocracy.

Still sozzled with jet lag that late afternoon,
Dumpty remained in his bedroom cocoon.
But a sudden and violent realization
Filled him with panic and disconsolation:

Transmogrifying from orange to gray,
He remembered too late it was Veterans Day!
He'd been so tormented, distracted, and nervous,
He'd blown yet another memorial service!

Spent with fatigue, perturbation, and dread,
Dumpty turned off the lights and crawled back into bed.
Thus ended six days of an unlucky streak
In his terrible, horrible, very bad week.

Next day, Dumpty struggled to lighten his mood
By turning to Twitter, Fox News, and junk food.
But befuddled, embittered, and racked with frustration,
He weighed other options for self-stimulation.

He wanted a rally! He wanted a crowd!
He wanted ovations, earsplittingly loud!
But with midterm campaigns having finished at last,
His rallies for now were a thing of the past.

He wanted a summit! A one-on-one chat
With a Russian, Korean, or Turk autocrat!
But summits are organized months in advance,
Not hastily launched by the seat of his pants.

"A Mack truck," Dumpty whimpered, a little forlorn.
"I could sit in the cab. Maybe play with the horn."
But trucks, he conceded, were not that much fun,
And the shtick with the horn had already been done.

One diversion remained as an apt last resort:
He could fire an official, if only for sport.
But while cheerfully weighing which victim to choose,
His contentment was shaken by late-breaking news:

The first lady, by custom so passive and meek,
Had shown a surprising tyrannical streak.
Proving herself a remorseless downsizer,
She had shit-canned a national security advisor.

Of all of the woes with which Dumpty was cursed,
Melania's action was plainly the worst.
Forget about Whitaker, France, and the rest:
His wife had outdone him at what he did best!

With another day lost to despondence and gloom,
Dumpty called for a steak to be sent to his room.
Despite all the perks and the trappings of power,
He ached for the haven of humble Dump Tower.

His supper arrived, but with no appetite
He sat in the fading, crepuscular light.
In the grips of a deadening, deepening funk,
He had to admit being president stunk.

He was seized by a thought that he couldn't dislodge:
"To hell with this crap! I'll just get outta Dodge!"
He could quit, as the liberal press had beseeched him;
Or sit back and watch while the Congress impeached him;

Or cop to each crime, each affair, and each fiction
And submit to Bob Mueller's impending conviction.
Incarceration? How bad could it be?
He would vastly prefer it to life in D.C.

But these musings had broken down Dumpty's defenses.
He quickly regrouped and came back to his senses.
Though "more of the same" made him inwardly squirm,
He was bound and determined to serve out his term.

"I'm the greatest!" he blustered, his swagger intact.
"I'm equipped with what all other POTUSes lacked!
I got through last week, I'll get through the duration!"
(Words rarely spoken elsewhere in the nation.)

With feverish thoughts of the next morning's tweets,
Dumpty plumped up his pillow and pulled back his sheets.
His political squabbles and media fights
Had earned him a lifetime of long sleepless nights.

He gave himself over to tossing and turning,
Consumed by vindictiveness, envy, and yearning.
He would try to forget but would always remember
These last seven days of this dreadful November.

MATTHEW WHITAKER *was appointed as acting attorney general after Trump forced* **JEFF SESSIONS** *out of office. This prompted several legal challenges from Senate Democrats who argued that the appointment was unconstitutional.*

MIRA RICARDEL *was named U.S. deputy national security advisor in April 2018 but was forced out in November of that year when Melania Trump called for her firing after the two argued over seating during Mrs. Trump's trip to Africa.*

TRUMPTY DUMPTY: PART 3

Trumpty Dumpty wanted more power.
Legal constraints made him cranky and sour.
Revered institutions and customs could fall
As long as he got his preposterous wall.

He peevishly called for a government shutdown
With wages and services drastically cut down.
His folly came off as an unfunny joke
When thousands of federal workers went broke.

The face-off in Congress was not even close, he
Was handily snookered by Nancy Pelosi.
He angrily mounted a counterinsurgency,
Launching a spurious National Emergency.

Trumpty Dumpty thus had begun
His maniacal trashing of Article One.
He's a rampant gorilla, let loose from the zoo:
Your chief executive, working for you.

The longest U.S. government shutdown in history, and the second during the presidency of Donald Trump, occurred between December 22, 2018, and January 25, 2019. **NANCY PELOSI**, *elected Speaker of the U.S. House of Representatives after Democrats won control in the 2018 midterms, successfully resisted Donald Trump's attempts to leverage a government shutdown to secure funding for a border wall.*

THE MOSCOW CIRCUS

1

The circus arrives and from all over town
People rush to the Big Top and sit themselves down.
Hungry for spectacle, action, and laughter,
They put off their worries until the day after.

For children, the happiest moment by far
Is when clowns tumble out of a miniature car.
It's a giddy escape from their everyday humdrum:
"Where," they cry out, "did those people all come from?"

Now suppose that the clowns in this comic confection
Are characters drawn from the Russia connection.
The casting is perfect, whomever you choose.
Where did they come from? The six o'clock news.

2

The Big Top lights up, the calliope surges,
And sly Sergey Kislyak brightly emerges.
Close on his heels is Oleg Deripaska
With riches sufficient to buy back Alaska.

Two moony fools are the next on the stage:
That fop Roger Stone and that geek Carter Page.
Then a pair of buffoons with matching fat torsi:
Portly Rob Goldstone and plump Jerome Corsi.

And then, to a chorus of deafening cheers,
Natalia Veselnitskaya appears
With Maria Butina, her equal in glamour,
Released for the day from the federal slammer.

Michael Cohen climbs out but nobody reacts
Since he's featured in all of the previous acts.
And just when you think that things couldn't get loonier,
Who should appear but that clown *Donald Junior*!

3

Ten co-conspirators packed in a car
Is a fitting summation of where we all are.
The antic hilarity, fun, and excitement
Are sadly diminished with each new indictment.

We laugh at their pratfalls and fatuous patter,
But felonious treason is no laughing matter.
The state of the nation is fixed in a frown,
At least 'til the circus packs up and leaves town.

86

SERGEY KISLYAK is a Russian diplomat whose meetings with Donald Trump's campaign advisors were a subject of federal investigation. **OLEG DERIPASKA** *is a Russian oligarch and a major client of* **PAUL MANAFORT**, *with whom he reportedly had a $10 million annual contract to advance Russian interests in the United States.*

British publicist **ROB GOLDSTONE** *facilitated a meeting between Donald Trump Jr. and Russian lawyer* **NATALIA VESELNITSKAYA** *to provide information beneficial to the Trump campaign.* **MARIA BUTINA** *is a Russian gun rights activist and alleged spy who pleaded guilty to charges that she acted as an illegal foreign agent.*

ROGER STONE, *a longtime Republican political strategist and Trump advisor, was arrested for witness tampering and lying to Congress about his foreknowledge of the release of the Clinton e-mails by WikiLeaks.* **JEROME CORSI** *was subpoenaed by the Mueller investigation due to his contacts with Roger Stone regarding WikiLeaks.* **CARTER PAGE** *was a foreign policy advisor for the Trump campaign but stepped down soon after news reports surfaced detailing his links with Russia.*

INDIVIDUAL ONE

He divided the country for profit and fun.
He's Individual One.

The lawyer and fixer for most of his crew
Was Individual Two.

The worst a campaign head could possibly be
Was Individual Three.

In less than a month, he was thrown out the door.
He's Individual Four.

A son who was taught to conceal and connive:
That's Individual Five.

The self-proclaimed King of Corrupt Dirty Tricks
Is Individual Six.

A daughter made use of to soften and leaven:
She's Individual Seven.

A scuzzy Breitbarter who's way overweight,
That's Individual Eight.

A son-in-law toeing the family line
Is Individual Nine.

A Russian seductress of NRA men,
She's Individual Ten.

The POTUS goes free but the rest are undone.
No career could survive such a ramshackle run.
They were finished before they had even begun.

Thanks a lot, Individual One.

Individual One: Donald Trump,
Individual Two: Michael Cohen,
Individual Three: Paul Manafort,
Individual Four: Michael Flynn,
Individual Five: Donald Trump Jr.,
Individual Six: Roger Stone,
Individual Seven: Ivanka Trump,
Individual Eight: Steve Bannon,
Individual Nine: Jared Kushner,
Individual Ten: Maria Butina.

ACOSTA AGONISTES

Alexander Acosta was doing just fine
  In his comfortable cabinet post.
Lucky for him, the Department of Labor
  Got far less attention than most.

Dumpty's first pick for Acosta's position
  Could hardly have been more obtuse:
Andy Puzder, renowned for his cheeseburger porno
  And rumors of spousal abuse.

Puzder was dumped in a clumsy debacle
  That pummeled the bumbling POTUS.
So Acosta, an amiable U.S. attorney,
  Drew virtually no public notice.

Scaramucci, Reince Priebus, Sean Spicer, and Bannon
    Were fired or forced to resign.
Fifty others all shared the same infamous fate,
    Yet Acosta was doing just fine.

But a ten-year-old story leaked out from his past
    And yanked him from placid obscurity.
His name was attached to a sickening scandal
    That shook his serene job security.

The law had caught up with a Palm Beach roué,
    A man of luxurious means,
Charged with trafficking, pimping, procuring, and rape
    Of dozens of underage teens.

He'd concocted a sexual pyramid scheme
    Of unspeakable breadth and perversity,
Promising vulnerable, penniless girls
    A route out of brutal adversity.

The perp, Jeffrey Epstein, deserved to be crushed
    By justice's ruthless iron fist,
But the priciest lawyers that money could buy
    Got him off with a slap on the wrist.

Life in prison? Oh no. A mere thirteen months
    In his own private wing of a jail,
With work release privileges twelve hours a day
    To relax and catch up on his mail.

In the history of flagrant miscarriage of justice,
  No case is as lurid and stark.
And the terms of the deal were kept under seal
  So the victims were kept in the dark.

Was a rigorous U.S. attorney in charge?
  Or a groveling, feckless imposter?
In fact, he heads up your Department of Labor:
  The amiable Alex Acosta.

A predator wed to a fawning enabler
  Is a fellowship forged by the devil.
Who would have thought such a partner in crime
  Would ascend to the cabinet level?

We are living, alas, in the Dumptyan Era
  Where scandals erupt by the hour.
They stir a recurring and queasy sensation,
  A virus infecting the health of the nation,
Brought on by a toxic and foul combination
  Of money, perversion, and power.

ANDREW PUZDER *was Donald Trump's first pick to serve as the U.S. secretary of labor, but Puzder withdrew when it became clear that the Senate, amid a backlash regarding his company's sexist ads and alleged labor law violations, wouldn't confirm him. To replace him,* **ALEXANDER ACOSTA,** *a former federal prosecutor in Florida, was nominated and confirmed for the position despite having approved a secret, lenient plea agreement for an influential financier and serial sex offender named* **JEFFREY EPSTEIN.**

HENTSY PENTSY

Hentsy Pentsy sat on a fence,
The most vapid and vacant of vice presidents.
A poem? Alas, at the end of the day
Quite frankly, dear reader, there's not much to say.

ANOTHER OWL, ANOTHER PUSSYCAT

(AFTER EDWARD LEAR)

1

The Owl and the Pussycat waged a war,
Attacking each other on Twitter.
The Owl would tweet from his toilet seat,
The Cat from his kitty litter.
"Little Rocket Man!" the Owl typed out,
Hurling infantile darts from afar.
The Pussy would shout, in a petulant pout,
"What a pitiful dotard you are,
You are,
You are!
What a pitiful dotard you are!"

2

But after a year of derision and smear
Their rancor gave way to expedience.
The two had their eyes on a joint Nobel Prize,
So they forged an accord of convenience.
Pussy wrote to the Owl, "You elegant fowl!
Let us meet where the Bong-Tree grows!"
He beguiled his old foe and with song sweet and low
Led him round by a ring in his nose,
His nose,
His nose,
Led him round by a ring in his nose.

3

In an unwelcome twist, their very next tryst
Brought an end to their infatuation.
It foundered on sanctions, on Otto Warmbier,
And, of course, on denuclearization.
In the course of their journey, the devious Puss
Had taken the Owl to school.
The delusional King of the Art of the Deal
Had come off as a bungling fool,
A fool,
A fool,
Had come off as a bungling fool.

KIM JONG-UN *has served as the supreme leader of North Korea since 2011. After trading insults with Donald Trump for months, he met with the president in June 2018 to discuss North Korea's nuclear program and again in February 2019. The two leaders did not reach an agreement.*

OTTO WARMBIER *was a college student from Ohio who was arrested by North Korean authorities for allegedly stealing a propaganda poster. While in custody, he suffered a brain injury and was returned to his family in a coma. Tragically, Warmbier passed away soon after.*

THE FOUR HORSEMEN OF FOXPOLITICS

Behold! The Four Horsemen of Foxpolitics!
Propaganda and might in an unholy mix.
Their right-wing agendas all nicely align:
Dumpty, Hannity, Murdoch, and Shine.

A POTUS, a pundit, a mogul, a shill,
Each Horseman excels at inciting ill will.
From Fox News, that encampment where chaos is king,
They've stabled their steeds in the White House West Wing.

At Fox, Bill Shine put his thumb on the scales
Protecting those horndogs O'Reilly and Ailes.
From there he suspended the world's disbelief
By protecting the rep of the horndog-in-chief.

Sean Hannity's rants grow increasingly eerie,
Embracing each crackpot conspiracy theory.
And once he dismounts from his nightly Fox rostrum,
He pitches the POTUS with each nutty nostrum.

Astride him rides Rupert, the newspaper czar,
The most barbarous media baron by far.
He's been granted a wish that he's never outgrown:
An American president all his own.

That would be Dumpty, the last of the Four
Whose obtuseness the others all try to ignore.
He strives to keep pace but he's sadly unable,
So he shovels the horseshit befouling their stable.

The nettlesome fact of the matter, alas, is
The fearsome Four Horsemen are four horse's asses
And masters of nothing but crass dirty tricks.
Behold! The Four Horsemen of Foxpolitics!

Chairman and CEO of Fox News **ROGER AILES** *resigned in July 2016 following sexual misconduct allegations. He was replaced by* **RUPERT MURDOCH**, *the co-chairman of Fox Corporation and executive chairman of News Corporation.*

BILL SHINE, *a former executive at Fox News, served as White House director of communications for Donald Trump for eight months before resigning to serve as an advisor on Trump's 2020 campaign.*

BILL O'REILLY *hosted* The O'Reilly Factor *on Fox News until he was fired in April 2017 after several sexual harassment settlements came to light.*

TRUMPTY DUMPTY: PART 4

Trumpty Dumpty wanted a barrier,
Broad as a wall but preferably scarier.
He wanted a fortress, forbidding and stout,
To keep all those meddling journalists out.

Dumpty detested each sentence they wrote.
Presidential harassment was getting his goat.
How could he counter their carping and slanders?
That impregnable bulwark, Sarah Huckabee Sanders.

In July 2017, **SARAH HUCKABEE SANDERS** *replaced* **SEAN SPICER** *as White House press secretary and frequently launched attacks on the "fake news" media in defense of President Donald Trump.*

MICHAEL D. COHEN

TO A RAT

(AFTER ROBERT BURNS)

Wee, cowerin', tim'rous, sweaty vermin,
Why the panic? Why the squirmin'?
I nae intend to preach a sermon
About thy spillin'.
Tho' thou sang like Ethel Merman,
We deem'd it thrillin'!

As Dumpty's fixer, life wa' sweet.
Thou'dst make 'em quake on ev'ry street.
Wi' towers o' gold and taxi fleet,
How high thou'dst climb!
But wi' thy neck 'neath Dumpty's feet,
Thou'dst crack in time.

For Dumpty sought to swell his pow'r,
Wi' thou beside him ev'ry hour,
Thy kinsmanship wast in full flow'r,
Thou wast content.
But Dumpty's pride would'st thee devour:
He pined for president!

When the scribes foresaw him losin',
Dumpty rashly sowed confusion
Sparkin' Putin's foul intrusion
Past all reason.
Subornin' unabashed collusion
Toyed wi' treason.

When Dumpty won, his skeevy past
Wa' boldly brought to light at last.
Each citizen wa' struck aghast
At thy complicity—
A shameful end, sae cruel and fast,
To thy felicity.

What punishment's as sharp as thine!
In prison clept, a hefty fine,
A brutal truth doth thee define,
Naught can belie:
The best laid plans o' rats and swine
Gang oft awry.

And yet, good rat, thy fate's a boon.
Three years in lockup endeth soon.
Thy hearings Dumpty did impugn,
Exposing all.
Thou ratted out a vile tycoon
And sped his fall!

MICHAEL COHEN *was the personal lawyer for Donald Trump from 2006 until May 2018. He was sentenced to three years in prison in December 2018 for violating campaign finance laws and for committing fraud and perjury.*

RANK-A-DANK-DANK

Rank-a-dank-dank,
Six men on a tank:
Rodrigo Duterte, Xi, Kim;
Jair Bolsonaro,
Mohammed bin Salman,
And Putin! Let's not forget him!

Their corrupt despotism
And shared barbarism
Are an ominous sign of our times.
They're perfect for doggerel
On themes demagoguerel,
Though hardly for lighthearted rhymes.

Their tyrannical acts
Include scuttling pacts
And peddling disinformation.
Plus they cruelly repress
Human rights and the press
By dabbling in assassination.

One fact that explains
Their bloodthirsty reigns
And the laws that they all circumvent
Is the loud validation,
Indeed exhortation,
Thrown out by our lout president.

But where *is* Dumpty, then,
'Midst these dastardly men?
He's there, but he's hidden inside.
Though at driving a tank
His skills are a blank,
He's taking them all for a ride.

Rank-a-dank-dank,
Six men on a tank,
Xi, Putin, and Kim to be sure;
Duterte, bin Salman,
Jair Bolsonaro,
And Dumpty, their hired chauffeur.

VLADIMIR PUTIN *(Russia),* **RODRIGO DUTERTE**
(Philippines), **XI JINPING** *(China),* **JAIR BOLSONARO**
(Brazil), **MOHAMMED BIN SALMAN** *(Saudi Arabia),*
and **KIM JONG-UN** *(North Korea) are known for their author-
itarian rules and questionable human rights records. At various
times, Donald Trump has been complimentary of each of them.*

AFTERWORD

The Report was at hand and Dumpty was manic,
Awash in a flood of distemper and panic.
At lush Mar-a-Lago, his Florida lair,
He braced for Bob Mueller, his ruthless Javert.
His heart skipped a beat when from distant D.C.
Came a call from Bill Barr, his conniving AG.
Dumpty lurched from his bed with a guttural groan
And with trembling fingers he picked up the phone.

"Great news!" Barr exclaimed. "We're home free! It's a wash!
The Report's a big nothing that's easy to quash!"
Thus began Barr's campaign to covertly impede it
Since he, only he, was permitted to read it.
In fact, he just gave it a cursory glance
But that hadn't thwarted his victory dance,
Nor forestalled his appalling misrepresentation
Proclaiming the POTUS's exoneration.

Dumpty shouted in triumph and leaped up elated.
Though blatantly guilty, he'd flagrantly skated.
But with Dumpty, elation takes curious forms,
He savages critics and ravages norms.
At such times he'll revert to his usual penchants:
Anger, malevolence, hatred, and vengeance.
So grabbing the throttle in both tiny hands,
He feverishly plotted his upcoming plans.

He'd suspend lots of rights to assert law and order;
Split up more families and shut down the border;
Stiff a few nations we've helped heretofore—
Guatemala, Honduras, and El Salvador;

Lean on producers to blackball his foes;
Cut climate protections to ghastly new lows;
Give Putin a pass on campaign interference
And get his best caddie security clearance.

If all of this fills you with shock and surprise,
Wake up, smell the coffee, and open your eyes.
He's done most of these things and a hundred things more,
And God only knows what he still has in store.
Sure, Dumpty's a foolhardy figure of fun,
But laugh at your peril: there's work to be done.
Democracy's frail but our spirit is firm:
Restrict Trumpty Dumpty to only one term.

ROBERT S. MUELLER *was appointed as the special counsel for the Department of Justice to oversee the investigation of Russian interference during the 2016 U.S. presidential election.*

WILLIAM BARR *was appointed as the U.S. attorney general in February 2019. His handling of special counsel Robert Mueller's report on the Russia investigation faced great scrutiny after the Democratic Party accused Barr of misleading the public in his testimony to Congress.*